Red Ridinghood

A pantomime

Book and lyrics by
David Cregan

Music and additional lyrics by
Brian Protheroe

Samuel French – London
New York – Sydney – Toronto – Hollywood

RED RIDINGHOOD

First presented at the Theatre Royal, Stratford East, London on 3rd December 1984, with the following cast of characters:

Mrs Nesta Ridinghood	Colin Bennett
George	Bob Critchley
Harold	James Saxon
Wolf	Michael Bertenshaw
Winifred	Ruth Sheen
Old Lemuel	Jim McManus
Gregory	Richard Lloyd-King
Hilda	Marjorie Yates
Thelma Ridinghood	Jo Warne
Red Ridinghood/Jenifer	Kate Hardie
Mr Orme	Colin Bennett
Alice	Anne Miles

Directed by Philip Hedley and Jonathan Martin
Designed by Gemma Jackson
Musical Direction by Robert Pettigrew

Prologue: Introducing Mr Charles

ACT I

Entr'acte: George and Harold lose a living

ACT II

MUSICAL NUMBERS

ACT I

1   Dum Diddle Aye Doo Dah
2   The Big Bad Wolf
3   A Life That Is Rash
4   The Worst, Though Loveliest
5   When A Girl Turns Into A Gran
6   What Are You Doing For Dinner Tonight?
7   Red Red Ridinghood
8   It's A Living
9   Maypole Song
9a Dance
10 I Cry Revenge

Entr'acte

11 The Wolf Rap
12 We Know Something

ACT II

12a George and Harold Recitative
13 Grandma's Call To Arms
14 A Basket of Goodies
15 Lantern Carol
15a Song Sheet (Grandma's Call To Arms)
16 I Blame Myself
17 Maypole Song (reprise)

The music for this pantomime is available from Samuel French Ltd

PROLOGUE*

George and Harold, both waiters, enter through the Audience

George A nice class of person here, Harold.

Harold A nice class of person here, George.

They arrive on stage

George And this is where he said to meet him.

Harold Yes.

George Well now, young ladies and young gentlemen, my name is George, and I am, as it were, in the feeding business.

Harold And my name is Harold, and I am also, as it might be, in the feeding business.

George And we work for our friend, Mr Charles.

Harold Mr Charles.

George Who has asked us to meet him here.

There is a sudden immense crash of thunder. The Lights go out and lightning flashes

The Wolf is revealed in a strange place, perhaps behind a gauze, and preferably only in outline

Wolf I am tired of eating old hens and clapped out rabbits!

Thunder is heard

George
Harold } *together* That's him, that's Mr Charles!

Wolf I am *not* losing my power! I am *not* growing old and flabby! But I must eat the best and most luscious food there is to show I am still strong and sleek!

Thunder is heard

Therefore, get me a juicy young person, preferably female, whom I can eat with pleasure as of yore.

George
Harold } *together* A young *person*?

Wolf (*impatient*) Yes, a girl, a girl, or a boy if you're stuck, and get on with it!

Thunder is heard again

---

*N.B. Paragraph 3 on page ii of this Acting Edition regarding photocopying and video-recording should be carefully read.

(*With dignity; e.g. Hamlet's Father*) I will now go to the wild and windy
marshes like my ancestors before me to wait for youuuuuuuuu!

The Wolf fades away in thunder, the Lights return to normal

George That was strange.
Harold He's never asked for anything like that before.
George It's always been old goats and mangy sheep.
Harold And occasionally a pensioner.
George Still, orders are orders, Harold.
Harold And times are very hard, so——
George⎫ *together* ⎰ We'd better find a juicy young person, or we'll be
Harold⎭   ⎱ out of work
George Now, behind here is a village, noted for its jolliness.
Harold And jolliness makes you juicy.
George So let's hope there are lots of jolly, juicy young persons here——
Harold All wanting to be eaten by a wolf.
George (*referring to the audience*) Though we can always raid the stalls if we
have to.

The gauze flies to reveal the village scene

Harold (*as the village is revealed*) Oh what a lot of jolliness is here!

ACT I

SCENE 1

The Village Green, with a seat and houses peeping out of the trees, run down but nice. It is very sunny

The Villagers, Old Lemuel, Gregory, Winifred and Hilda sing, while dancing with Morris equipment

Song 1: Dum Diddly Aye Doo Dah

All   We'm dum diddly-aye dooh dah as merry as Greeks,
We dum diddly-aye dance in this manner for weeks,
With tambours and hankies and shoes all ashine,
O dum diddley-aye dooh dah we'm up on cloud nine.

George and Harold become involved in the dance

Oh dum diddly-aye dooh dah dum diddly-aye dum doh,
We diddly-aye in rain and we diddly-aye in snow,
And if no-one stops us then we've heard it said
We'll dum diddly-aye dance till we diddly-aye drop dead.

George and Harold try to speak

Oh dum diddly-aye dooh dah, dum diddly-aye dum day,
For passing the time there is no better way,
And if you don't like it then dum diddly-aye dee,
It's a dum diddly-aye pity cos that's all there be.

Winifred (*to the audience*) There we are then, this is our very jolly village, and we've got visitors.
Old Lemuel
Gregory } *together* Hello, visitors.
Winifred We're all very nice here.
Hilda No, we're not.
Winifred Oh, we are, Hilda.

George shakes hands with everyone one at a time, feeling them with the hand that isn't used for shaking and dictating to Harold as he goes

George (*with Old Lemuel*) My friend and I are both very glad to hear it—stringy—(*with Winifred*) because we two gentlemen have just moved into the area—flabby—(*with Hilda*) and we're making what you might call a survey—tough as old boots—(*with Gregory*) since we work in the feeding business, as it were—Ah.

Gregory (*as George goes on feeling him*) What's all this?
George A possibility.
Harold A possibility.
Hilda A possibility?
George Not a great one, it's male.
Gregory Are you looking for an eager youth, then?
George ⎫
Harold ⎭ *together* Tender more than eager.

George and Harold laugh, and continue feeling Gregory

Hilda Lem, there's tweaking going on.
Old Lemuel Tweaking?
Hilda Look.
Old Lemuel Oh my lord and sainted aunt, there is.
Hilda The way you tell the stories of the Wolf Time there was always tweaking before—before——
Old Lemuel There was. (*To audience*) Back in the Wolf Time there was always tweaking and then—ugh.
Hilda Gregory, come here.
Gregory Whatever is it?
George Nothing's settled yet ma'am. We're seeing many people in this matter, girls especially.
Harold What's that?

A row has broken out off stage

Winifred That's the Ridinghood family. (*To the audience*) Very nice people, if high spirited.
Hilda Winifred, hold your tongue.

Jenifer enters, a messy tomboy carrying a hammer and some messy bright notices and bunting laid on a folded step ladder

Thelma, Jenifer's mother, enters, holding the other end of the ladder

Jenifer When you're making decorations some things do get smashed but I haven't smashed anything that matters *at all*.
Thelma (*speaking at the same time*) You always make excuses Jenifer, and you always smash everything, (*in tears*) EVERYTHING, EVERYTHING. (*To the audience, letting go her end of the ladder*) Oh, she gives me a headache.
Jenifer You dropped it.
Old Lemuel Have a drop of Old Lem's Dratted Pick-Me-Up, Thelma, while I talk to you private. (*He tries to talk to the weeping Thelma unsuccessfully*)
Winifred (*to the audience*) Now that's Mrs Ridinghood, Thelma, had a lot of trouble in her life and widowed with it.
Gregory So she says.
Winifred She is, Gregory.
Jenifer (*ascending the ladder to nail things in*) And I'm her daughter, Jenifer

Ridinghood, and I'm imaginative, and I'm difficult, (*to the Waiters*) and I don't like the look of you.

Jenifer pushes the approaching George and Harold out of the way

Hilda (*coming between Jenifer and the men*) They're a single parent family and we have a duty to look after them.
Winifred (*surprised at the kind thought*) Oh, Hilda!
Jenifer Furthermore, tomorrow is Grandma's Party Day which Grandma gives us all once a year, and I'm putting up the decorations and you're standing on them.
George ⎫
Harold ⎭ *together* Oh—oh——
Jenifer Thank you. (*She pulls some bunting free*) Go on talking all of you.
George Rather gristly, don't you think?

Jenifer bangs loudly with the hammer, putting the notice into the tree

Thelma (*holding her head*) Oh, oh! I hate Grandma!
Jenifer What!
Thelma (*in tears*) She always says I'm dreary and miserable.
Jenifer Well you are dreary and miserable.

Before Jenifer finishes, Thelma rushes at her. There is a big confrontation. The following speeches are spoken together

Thelma Jenifer, you're not to talk to your mother like that, it's rude, it's terribly rude, and when I think of all the time and trouble spent on trying to make you a lady, well, a silk purse out of a sow's ear isn't in it, boohoo, (*ad infinitum*)
Jenifer I'll talk to my mother how I like if she calls the only person who's any fun in our lives a terrible person, because she isn't, she's lovely and I like her better than you.

While all this is happening the others are separating the antagonists and saying soothing things. Winifred has gone instantly to call—

Winifred Mr Orme, Mr Orme, Mr Orme!

Mr Orme appears, a balding watch-chained banker

Orme Now, now, now, now. Peace! We're all very jolly here.

There is peace

George Funny people, Harold.
Harold Funny people, George.
Winifred (*to the audience*) Mr Orme's the bank manager, and very stable.
Old Lemuel Very pompous.
Winifred He isn't, Lemuel.
Orme (*to Thelma*) Now, my little dream of happiness, stop sniffing for your bank manager, and Jenifer, stop sulking and smile sweetly.

Thelma stops crying and Jenifer smiles

George Oh, she looks almost tasty when she smiles.
Harold She does.

They go to tweak Jenifer

Old Lemuel Stop. You're tweakers, aren't you?
Hilda Own up and tell us.
Harold George, they've taken, as it were, against us.
George (*backing off*) Yes. We don't know what a tweaker is, madam.
Harold We're simply in the feeding business.
George Which is a living.
Harold Yes, a living.
George ⎫
Harold ⎬ *together* So excuse us while we get on with our work.
Gregory You won't forget me?
Hilda Gregory, come here.
Harold Don't call us, we'll call you.
George Let's see if the livestock's any better.

George and Harold go

Orme Who were those men?
Old Lemuel (*coming forward*) Tweakers, I'll swear by the Old Dratted Pick-Me-Up.
Winifred Oh Lem, tweakers, what on earth are tweakers?
Old Lemuel (*as the Ancient Mariner; to the audience and everyone*) Hark and listen while I tell you about the tweakers who came in the dreaded Wolf Time.
Jenifer Oh great!

Atmospheric music is heard

Old Lemuel It is the curse of our village that every sixty years, give or take a few, at the time of the scudding moon, more or less, there comes out there upon the Wild and Windy Marshes——
All (*including the audience*) Ooooh!
Old Lemuel A Wolf!
All (*including the audience*) A Wolf!
Old Lemuel Who eats the very best that's going.
Gregory Oh.
Old Lemuel The last time he came I was a little lad of ten, and your grandmother was twelve, and he raged and savaged all about till Great Grandfather Ridinghood killed him dead as dead. There. That's it.

The music stops

Hilda The tweakers, Lemuel.
Old Lemuel Oh! That's not it.

The music sounds again

Every day, the Wolf sent out two tweakers, who tweaked away to find the

choicest meat. And when they found it, the Wolf came down and ate it, with groans and moans and ugh and yuk.
All (*including the audience*) Ergh!
Old Lemuel There, that *is* it.

The music stops

Jenifer Fabulous.
Hilda And those two have been tweaking here today.
Old Lemuel They have.
Gregory Did they want me for a wolf, then?
Old Lemuel Mayhap.
Jenifer Wow! How marvellous!
Thelma Don't be ridiculous, Jenifer.
Gregory And there could be a wolf out there, now, thinking about me?
Old Lemuel There could.
Jenifer Wonderful, Greg!
Gregory Is it? What was he like, then, the last one that came?
Jenifer I'll tell you exactly what he was like because I can just imagine him.
Old Lemuel (*tetchily*) It's my story.

Song 2: The Big Bad Wolf

Jenifer	He prowled about on enormous paws,
	With loads of old bones dripping out of his jaws,
	His eyes were like plates that have never been clean,
	Which flickered and flashed in a heejus green.
All	Oooh-ooh-ooh.
	Aaah-aah-aah.
Jenifer	He'll slobber and gobble,
	Be nothing but trouble,
	The Big Bad Wolf.
Orme	His teeth were like tent pegs all yellow and black,
	And fleas big as rats were all over his back,
Hilda	The sound from his mouth was a crack and a crunch,
	As he chewed up a couple of goats for lunch.
All	Oooh-ooh-ooh.
	Aaah-aah-aah.
Orme ⎫	⎧ He'll slobber and gobble
Hilda ⎬ *together*	⎨ Be nothing but trouble
Jenifer ⎭	⎩ The Big Bad Wolf.
Jenifer	His tail when wagging made tremors and shocks.
Winifred	He stood over twenty foot high in his socks.
Old Lemuel	His forehead was covered in ice and snow.
Thelma	And dozens were crushed under each big toe.
All	Ooh-ooh-ooh.
	Aah-aah-aah.

He'll slobber and gobble,
Be nothing but trouble,
The Big Bad Wolf.

Our hair is stiff to the roots,
Our hearts are throbbing in our boots,
If one should come again today,
We wonder whether we'd run away.

His belly was one of the larger caves,
With juices all swilling around in waves,
And all of us here would go down in a gulp,
And drown in the terrible slimy pulp.

Ooh-ooh-ooh.
Aah-aah-aah.

He'll slobber and gobble,
Be nothing but trouble,
The Big Bad Wolf.

At the end of the song, the sky darkens, thunder is heard. There is a great growl—not too close—and lightning

Jenifer There! There is a wolf! And I'll bet he's coming this way!
Gregory Because he knows about me.
Jenifer I should think so. Come on, it's wolf-ridding time and I'm in charge.
Orme As manager of the local branch of——
Jenifer Arm yourselves with anything you can so we'll be ready for him. Hurry, we probably haven't got long.

Winifred ⎫
Hilda ⎬ *together variously* { Right oh. Well I never did *etc.*
Old Lemuel ⎭

Winifred, Hilda and Old Lemuel go

Gregory I'll stay near you, Jenifer.

Gregory and Jenifer go

Orme Have this whistle, Thelma of my dreams. It's property of the bank.

Mr Orme goes

Thelma I've no blow.

George and Harold return

George (*looking at the list*) One scrawny donkey, four ancient turkeys and a couple of mouldy geese.

Harold points to the darkening sky. There is a flash of lightning and a low rumble of thunder

Harold George look! The Wolf Weather. It's coming this way.

George It's Mr Charles. He's lost his cool again. You know what that means.

Harold He messes everything up and we get hunted all over the place.

George Let's clear out before anyone sees us.

George and Harold head back through the audience, talking as they go

Harold You'll have to speak to him about this sort of thing.

George Why is it always me?

Thelma (*realising that George and Harold are the tweakers*) Mr Orme, Mr Orme, those men!

Mr Orme enters, carrying an army revolver

Orme You blow your whistle if you need me.

Thelma I've lost it.

Orme (*alarmed*) It's the property of the bank.

There is a sudden vast, blood-curdling roar, lots of lightning and thunder. Thelma throws her apron over her face and cries

Jenifer, Gregory, Winifred, Hilda, and Old Lemuel rush back in, armed. Winifred has a Red Cross box

Jenifer Wowee!

The Wolf is apparently at the back of the stage—though no-one can quite see him

Wolf, wherever you are, we aren't afraid of you. We've got weapons and things!

The Wolf roars again

Old Lemuel Where is he?

Gregory (*nervously*) Can he smell me?

Jenifer Shout, all of you, to make him think there's lots of us.

They all shout "Boo". The great roar returns at the climax

Jenifer (*to the audience*) You too. Come on. Louder, louder. That's it. Louder. Try this. Wolf, Wolf, go away, we don't want you any day.

Winifred Oh, that's lovely.

Gradually the roar fades. The sky clears. Birds sing

Jenifer He's gone (*With sudden annoyance*) How boring, it's absolutely wolfless now.

Gregory Cowardly old Wolf! See if I care!

Hilda We did it, though, Jenifer. We won.

Winifred (*indicating the audience*) And them. Thank you ever so much.

All Yes. Yes, thank you.

Jenifer (*pleased again*) Yes, well done all of us. And he's bound to come back.

Gregory He's not!

Jenifer That's the best part of it, Greg, he will come back, and this time we'll be really ready for him. Pow! Wow!

Hilda By George we will, and then once more unto the breach dear friends, once more!

Winifred Good heavens, Hilda.

Jenifer You've understood me at last, Hilda. I'm not really difficult, am I? I just believe excitement is everything.

Orme Well, there is much to be said for the quiet steady way of doing things.

Song 3: A Life that is Rash

Jenifer

You've always lived a life of calm,
Sitting at your ease,
Far from danger, safe from harm
Under the summer trees.
But now you've felt a different feeling,
Heard excitement call,
And you can understand me when
I tell this to you all. Give me a—

Life that is rash,
Packed with daring and dash,
Filled to bursting with catastrophes galore;
Where witches with cats
Whistle round you like bats,
Deadly dragons flock in dozens round the door;

A life that explodes
With magicians and toads,
Where there's hoards of hungry giants roaming free;
On a sunny day like this,
That is my idea of bliss,
It's exciting and inviting and it's me!

A life that is rough,
Full of horrors and stuff,
Where there's mighty genies darkening the sky;
And ogres with maces,
And knobs on their faces,
Can squash you in the twinkling of an eye;

Where vampires so gruesome
Can break up a twosome
By swooping down and calling in for tea;
On a sunny summer's day,
These are games I want to play,
They're exciting, they're inviting and they're me!

All   One heck of a life,
              Filled with wonderful strife,
              Where the Beauty's always running from the Beast;
              And roaring down stairs
              Come those great grizzly bears
              Wanting Goldie to pay plenty for her feast;

              Where frightened Aladdin
              Is half going mad in
              The cave his uncle sealed him in with glee;
              On a sunny day like this, that is my idea of bliss
              It's inviting and it's what I long to be;
              It's exciting and it's absolutely me!

Jenifer Great. Now let's make a list of people to do guard duty. (*She goes to Gregory, Old Lemuel and Hilda*)

Thelma (*beginning to leave*) It's all brought on my headache, so I'll go and have a lie down.

Orme offers Thelma some pills as they start to leave

Orme Have an aspirin, little mother.
Thelma You're very comforting.
Orme It's the training at head office.

   Orme and Thelma leave

Hilda (*to the audience*) He carries on with her, you know
Winifred He doesn't, Hilda. They've just been engaged for seven years, that's all.

   Hilda and Winifred leave

Jenifer Goodness, Grandma's Party. I'd forgotten Grandma's Party. You two get ready to bring her safely through the woods tomorrow morning, far deep in the heart of the forest.

Gregory But he knows about me.
Old Lemuel Wolves always sleep late, don't worry.
Jenifer And you'll be safe if you bring her by the big broad path. Wolves never go that way.
Old Lemuel Yes, the big broad path. Wolves never go that way.
Jenifer Tonight I'll see if I can find the Famous A Number One Wolf Trap from last time. Wow. I wonder what it's like out there on the Wild and Windy Marshes. I wish I was there with him. I'd show him!

   Jenifer, Old Lemuel and Gregory exit

Fade to Black-out

SCENE 2

Mr Charles Explains Himself

The stage is dark. The sound of wind rises to barely tolerable proportions. The sound of the Wolf cries grow louder and louder

These are the Wild and Windy Marshes

Gradually moonlight shows through the scudding clouds and reveals the Wolf pacing round and round the stage, eyes gleaming and claws flashing. He bays the moon. Then he calls

Wolf My slaves! Where are my slaves?

George and Harold enter

George Here we are, Mr Charles.
Harold At your service, Mr Charles, O Wolf, sir.
Wolf Aaaah!
George Someone was a naughty Wolf, weren't they? Going out among the populace. Ooops!

The Wolf lunges at George, who dodges. Harold hides behind George

Harold Oh George.
Wolf You kept me waiting and waiting and waiting, and I'm famous for my impatience. What've you found?
George Well, there's a rather gristly girl and some old yokels.
Wolf (*in anguish*) Nooooo!
Harold You've eaten gristly girl and old yokel before.
Wolf But never again, I've told you! I want and I must have, a superb experience, tender to the tongue and sweet to the tooth, to show I'm still the best.
George There's one or two quite pleasing little things out there.
Harold Though they don't like you much by the sound of it.
Wolf I wouldn't stoop to them. And I want to be alone with my victim, to make it run around in terror, and then I'll catch it and claw it into little pieces and munch it and crunch it and slobber over it and drool and be generally disgusting. (*He has to wipe his mouth*)
George I see.
Harold (*ironically*) Lovely.
Wolf I am the Wolf of Wolves! And I've come here like my ancestors before me to prove I'm still the savagest there is, with the shiniest of claws and the yellowest of eyes and the most appalling habits!
George
Harold } *together* All right, all right, just give us time.

Song 4: The Worst, Though Loveliest

Wolf (*Singing*) I know I've been the most awful of all,
                                    As a cub I wanted to be.

I could always eat from the tenderest meat,
But now it's eluded me.
So a monstrous tummy ache is taunting me loud,
"You must feed as you did once again!"
For the worst though loveliest of all the beasts
Is hungry for the best of men!

*In the second verse wolfish silhouettes appear with illuminated yellow eyes to
howl in harmony with the Wolf. Mist appears around them*

I call on all of my ancestors wild
Just to send me a victim pure,
Some fair young soul I can savour with joy,
As I swallow down the skin once more.
For I'm mighty weary of the ticky tacky bones
Of the cart horse, the donkey and hen.
I'm the worst though loveliest of all the beasts,
And I'm hungry for the best of men.

When a wolf has done what a wolf has to do,
And the history books tell of his fame,
In the hall of the great there will stand in state
A bust of him bearing his name,
And beneath these words etched in letters of gold
Will flame over mountain and fen,
"He was the worst, though loveliest, of all the beasts—
We shall never see his like again!
He was chosen, he was best, he succeeded in his quest,
To feed upon the best of men!"

The Wolf exits

Harold Leave it to us, just leave it to us.
George To us, you understand, to us.

George and Harold head for the audience

Come on Harold, let's get away where we can watch out for someone.
Harold I expect the next thing we watch will be Grandma waking up
tomorrow morning in the heart of the forest. There. I said so.
George Very vertical places, forests.

George and Harold exit

Scene 3

*Grandma's cottage, interior or exterior. It is severe yet extravagant, the
cottage of an Edwardian lady*

Grandma (*off*) Alice? Alice, time to do my stays. Alice?

The elegant and tough Grandma Ridinghood enters, in a lovely night cap and dressing gown, the cap hiding a blonde Veronica Lake hair do

Oh, servants, never where you want them at great expense. Never mind, my dears, hello. I'm Grandma, Mrs Nesta Ridinghood, retired, of Throstling Side, Dingle Hollow, the Forest, a small place, but my own, and you're very, very welcome. Alice! My stays. Little scatterbrain. I have to have my stays done up especially tightly today, so that I look bewilderingly beautiful when I visit the village. I'm taking a present to my gorgeous granddaughter, whom I adore beyond belief. Have you seen her? Isn't she a pet? Oh she is. If a bit rough. As a matter of fact, the present I'm taking her is going to change all that. It's a lovely red cloak — a Red Ridinghood, ha, ha, ha, ha! I must show you. Alice? The present.

Alice rushes on, all of a dither

Alice Oh, Mrs Ridinghood Senior, ma'am, I've met Lem and Greg and Winifred in the wood coming to collect you, and oh, ma'am, it's Wolf Time again.
Grandma No it isn't.
Alice Yes it is, it is.
Grandma No it's not, it's not.
Alice But ma'am.
Grandma I will not have any mention of Wolf Time anywhere near me, d'you understand?
Alice But ma'am ...
Grandma I've known Wolf Time, and when it happens there are no sweets, no pretty clothes, everyone gets in a bother and behaves badly.
Alice But ma'am...
Grandma So it's not Wolf Time, it's Grandma's Summer Party Time and it's Present for Jenifer Time, and that's final.
Alice Yes, ma'am.
Grandma (*to the audience*) Wolf Time. Throw a wolf a bag of bacon rind and he slobbers off with his tail wagging. No taste at all. Life, Alice, is joy and beauty.
Alice Yes ma'am.
Grandma (*taking off her dressing gown*) And that is me, joy and beauty to the core.
Alice You had better get a move on with your joy and beauty, ma'am, or you won't be dressed when the others come.

Grandma is revealed in a corset with the stays hanging loose

Grandma I need to lose six inches in ten seconds.
Alice We'll do it, ma'am, we'll do it.

Grandma braces herself. Alice grabs at the stays

Grandma Come on then, after three, when I breathe in. Ready?
Alice Yes.

Grandma One—two—three!
Alice Heave!

Grandma breathes in while Alice heaves and urges her on

That's all ma'am.
Grandma (*through clenched teeth*) Right then. One more time.

The business is repeated. Alice is now slipping and sliding but hanging on

Grandma (*breath held, teeth clenched*) Hold it! We've got there! Alice, tie it up quick!
Alice I will, I will, I will! I'm doing it, I'm doing it—I've done it! You can breathe.

Grandma exhales, then stands in some stiff splendour

Grandma Behold, a nodding lily flower in its first flush.
Alice Oh you look so graceful ma'am. (*To the audience*) Doesn't she look graceful?
Grandma Oh you're too kind, but I know it's true, and I wish some of you were older. No dear, not you. Alice, the rest of my clothes please, and the present. And my pills in case I go funny.

Alice goes to fetch these

Old Lemuel (*off*) Yoohoo! Mrs Ridinghood Senior!
Winifred (*off*) We've come to take you safely to the village.
Grandma (*snatching up a housecoat or something*) Oh my goodness, hurry Alice!
Gregory (*off*) Are you ready?
Grandma No, I'm not dressed!
Gregory (*off*) You're not what?

Winifred, Gregory and Old Lemuel enter

Old Lemuel I've brought you a drop of the Old Dratted to help you on— ooooooh, my Sainted Aunt! (*He wheels away in a fluster and drinks deeply*)

Gregory wanders around behind Grandma

Gregory Oh my goodness. You're all done up like a sausage, aren't you.

Alice enters with Grandma's clothes

Alice Gregory! (*She slaps Gregory's face. To everyone*) We're sweethearts.
Grandma (*flinging aside the housecoat*) Oh, let him look his fill, Alice, and see the effort that goes into civilization.
Winifred Doesn't it hurt?
Grandma It does. But older people have a duty to look beautiful.
Winifred Do you?
Grandma Yes we do!

Song 5: When a Girl Turns Into a Gran

*Note: Grandma dresses or is dressed either during the song or the chorus.
Obviously it is an integral part of the song, but can be fitted in how best works*

(*Singing*)   You may laugh at poor old me,
                     Trussed up in this way,
                     But I believe that Grannies
                     Have a calling to obey.

                     They *must* set an example,
                     In a world that droops with care,
                     And show the young things how to carry
                     Life along with flair.

                     When a girl turns into a gran,
                     It's her duty to do what she can,
                     To brush up the truth
                     Of her vanishing youth
                     With a frou-frou, a fur or a fan.
                     She must squash her size nines into pumps,
                     So you don't see the knobs and the bumps,
                     Make the fat bits look thin,
                     And pad out what's gone in
                     When a girl turns into a gran.

All   When a girl turns into a gran,
                     She should use the inventions of man,
                     If the blooms on her cheek
                     Have begun to look bleak
                     She can spray new ones on from a can.
                     If she needs a smile none can surpass,
                     There it is, by her bed, in a glass,
                     And the bump round her ear
                     Means at least she can hear
                     When a girl turns into a gran.

                     If time's horny finger is wagging
                     Don't whine at the sign that you're old

Grandma   You can sew up the bits that are sagging
                     And turn back the silver to gold!

*Here Grandma pulls off her mob cap and her Veronica Lake blonde hair-do
swings into place*

All   For a grandma can show how to win,
                     She's a dame who is game for a spin,

Grandma   She can dance the night through
                   Looking—what?; thirty-two,
All   If her Guinness is topped up with gin.

> With the help of a corset and gown,
> She can burn every head in the town,
> And be voted the tops
> Till the moment she drops—

Pause. All droop, cough, smile firmly again

> When a girl turns into
> A girl turns into
> A girl turns into a gran! To a gran!

Winifred Oh you look lovely, Mrs Ridinghood Senior, you really do.

Grandma (*Now fully dressed in her war paint*) Thank you, Winifred, and I'm sure I can teach Jenifer how to look lovely too, despite the efforts of her unfortunate mother, that chewed over sponge, Thelma, my waterlogged daughter.

Winifred Thelma's had a lot of trouble in her life, Mrs Ridinghood Senior.

Grandma And there's more on the way.

  (*Singing*)   Oh a Gran may look happy and gay,
> But she knows how to get her own way.
> She's a terror to some
> For she's tough as they come,
> When a girl turns into a Gran!

A dogcart is brought in

Grandma mounts the dogcart

Grandma exits in the dogcart, like Boadicea

SCENE 4

George and Harold's Invitation

A front cloth

George and Harold come up on stage

George Is that everyone, d'you think?

Harold It seems like it.

George Well there's nothing for him there. He wants a real chef's delight, a proper cheeky little chubby chops he can slobber over.

Harold Even the maid had knobbly knees and he always chokes on those.

George We must persevere further, then, Harold, or we shall lose our living.

Harold And we can't do that.

George   ⎱
             together No. So——
Harold   ⎰

Song 6: What are you doing for Dinner Tonight?

(*Singing*)   We're looking for a supper,
A toothsome trim and sweet,
A charming little person who
Is very good to eat.
And when we come upon them
Amid life's happy throng,
You'll hear us warble merrily
This chatty little song.

Oh, what are you doing for dinner tonight?
We know an under-rated place
Where you can get a bite.
It's perhaps a trifle drafty,
The owner's dressed in furs
But if he really takes to you
He grins at you and purrs.
Then rather unexpected is the
Service that occurs,
So join us for dinner tonight.

Improvisation follows, with members of the audience who are eligible, e.g.: "A sizzled senior citizen", "A toasted toddler", "That one must taste good, he's eating his fingernails", etc. This leads to picking out one person: "Ooh look! He's the one for us!"

Oh, what are you doing for dinner tonight?
Your presence at our table would
Be really quite a sight.
Your cheeks are oh so tempting
And delicious are your eyes
Your colour is mouth watering—
No artificial dyes—
And most of all, my darling,
You are just the perfect size
To join us for dinner
And stop him getting thinner,
So join us for dinner tonight!

George So let's see what happens next then, Harold, and hope for the best.
Harold There's always hope, George.
George But not much ...

George and Harold exit

SCENE 5

A Red Riding Hood arrives

The village. Barricades are mixed with "Welcome to Grandma" notices; also "Wolf keep out" notices

Mr Orme is pacing up and down with a revolver. Thelma is with him, holding her whistle

Thelma All this fuss, Mr Orme. It's awful.

Orme It will end one day, apple of my eye.

Thelma And Grandma's coming, too. I wish I'd never met her.

Orme She's your mother.

Thelma Yes, I know. (*She is in tears*)

Orme When the Wolf Time is over, cherub of my heart, I will whisk you away from your family no matter what, and we'll be man and wife together.

Thelma Oh, Roger!

Orme Oh, Thelma!

Grandma (*off*) Yoo hoo!

Grandma and Alice enter

Jenifer, Winifred, Hilda, Gregory and Old Lemuel enter from a different direction

Jenifer (*running round the stage*) She's here! Grandma's here! Oh wow, wow, wowow!

Grandma Hello. Hello!

Jenifer Grandma! Weeeeeeeeee! (*She flings her arms round Grandma's neck*)

Grandma Oh my dear, dear granddaughter! You're the greatest pleasure a lady could hope for at a certain age.

Jenifer And you're the best thing that ever happened. Except for the Wolf of course. We're having a marvellous time with him as you can see from the barricades and——

Grandma Stop! I will not hear one word about any of that today, Jenifer.

Jenifer But Grandma, it's fun!

Grandma It's boring.

Jenifer It isn't boring.

Hilda We have to be prepared for this wolf, Mrs Ridinghood Senior.

Grandma Oh nothing's going to eat you Hilda, so don't get excited.

Jenifer But Grandma——

Hilda (*to the audience*) Tell her there's a wolf, go on tell her.

Grandma Oh no there isn't!

Audience Oh yes there is!

Grandma (*taking the whistle from Thelma and blowing it*) Now not another word about wolves. Today is my Party Day. (*Whispering*) And there's Jenifer's present.

Thelma You've found my whistle, mother.

Grandma Ah, Thelma. (*Throwing the whistle back*) Trying to turn frogs into princes, are we?

Jenifer Grandma——

Thelma Mother, please. . . .

Grandma You know I don't approve of Mr Orme. He's got no flair, no style, no snap to his garter, and you're not to marry him.

Orme Mrs Ridinghood Senior, we are quite old enough to——

Grandma And now you're going to cry, aren't you?

Thelma (*trying not to*) No I'm not!

Jenifer (*outraged*) Grandma!

Grandma (*to the audience*) She is, she's going to cry.

Thelma I'm not——

Grandma You are——

Thelma I'm not——

Grandma You are——

Thelma I'm not!

Grandma Go on, cry!

Thelma cries

(*To the audience*) There, I told you, she's crying. I don't know how I gave birth to such a little storm cloud.

Jenifer Grandma, that was horrid.

Grandma Was it? Oh diddlums diddlums, cheery-up 'ems. (*Handing her handkerchief to Thelma*) Blow your beastly nose, Thelma, and stop spoiling things. I have brought my granddaughter a present. Alice.

Alice Yes, ma'am.

Alice goes to get the present

Jenifer A present.

Grandma A present to beat all presents.

Jenifer Something for fighting wolves, wow, pow!

Grandma Certainly not! I mean—Jenifer, I do sometimes wonder about your clothes.

Thelma I wouldn't use them to wash up in.

Winifred Oh you would, Thelma.

Grandma So I've brought you a little something which I think might just take your fancy.

Alice enters, holding a beautifully wrapped gift

Alice Oh it will, I know it will, it's just swoony.

Jenifer (*tearing away at the wrapping*) Gran, it looks fabulous.

Hilda Frivolous, you mean.

Grandma Yes.

Jenifer I hope it's a pair of dungarees, or one of those aprons where you can put everything you need into pockets. OH! (*She shows great disappointment as she reveals a lovely red cloak and white dress and red shoes*)

Gregory Oh, it's lovely, Jenifer.

Thelma Have you brought me a present, Mother?

Grandma No, of course I haven't. What d'you think of it, my darling?

Jenifer Well—perhaps Mother would like it instead, as it's not really me.

Grandma Of course it's you. Please Jenifer, sweetheart, just for me, try it on

and see what you think. Then if you don't like it, soppy Thelma can have
it, I promise you.

Thelma Yes, go on, Jenifer.

All (*except Hilda*) Yes, do, etc.

Grandma And when you see yourself in the mirror—Alice—you might get
the surprise of your life.

*Alice exits and re-enters immediately, wheeling on a large object covered
with a pretty cloth*

Jenifer All right. Just for you Gran. (*She kisses Grandma*)

Grandma Dear girl.

Jenifer goes behind the object

The angel. So like myself when young—youn*ger*.

Old Lemuel (*gurgling*) Ah hahahahaha.

Grandma Oh you remember, do you, Lemuel?

Thelma She won't see herself in any mirror because she's broken every one
we have in the house. Thirty five years' bad luck, that's what we've got.

Orme My little tragic heroine.

*Grandma pulls off the cloth to reveal a great gilt mirror behind which Jenifer is
changing*

Grandma I've brought one of my own.

Gregory (*peacocking*) Oh, it's lovely.

Hilda There's a wolf out there, Gregory, and it knows about you. This is all
nonsense at a time like this.

Grandma No, it's fun, Hilda.

Winifred Will she come out all ladylike then?

Grandma Sh!

*The following song and verse are sung quietly so as not to alert Jenifer to what
Grandma intends, and what the others all expect to happen*

Song 7: Red Red Ridinghood

Grandma (*speaking*) Prepare yourselves for a wonderful surprise,
Stopping up your breath and blinding all your eyes,
For I have planned that Jenifer will now appear to
you,
The perfect dream of youth and girlish loveliness
come true,

In her—

(*Singing*) Red Red
Red Ridinghood
Jaunting, flaunting
Bright and stridinghood—

No more childish pranks,
She's a fully grown Ridinghood girl

Red Red
Red Ridinghood,
Full of charm and
Sweet confidinghood
Watch those colours glow
As her butterfly wings unfurl.

All   She'll be sweet to look at in
The silk and the satin,
Delightful, and demure,
She'll win every part of
The glittering heart of
The world of *haute couture*.

Oh Red Red
Red Ridinghood,
Play the game of
Seek and hidinghood,
Be that girl that everyone wants to adore,
Grandma   And love Red Ridinghood
For evermore.

Jenifer appears wearing the new clothes. She walks however in a very butch and gawky manner. The music goes on

Jenifer Well, here it is Grandma and it's absolutely ghastly. Mother, you'd better have it. I'll get back to the Wolf Trap.
Grandma (*leading Jenifer to the mirror*) The mirror, my love.
Jenifer It's no use, I know it's ghastly without looking in that. (*She does so*) Oh! (*She is very taken with herself*)
Grandma (*arranging the clothes*) Just straighten your back and smile, slightly.

Jenifer obeys these instructions

Thelma Oh she's lovely, Roger.
Gregory Isn't she just?
Alice Gregory?
Grandma Head to one side.
Jenifer Goodness.
Winifred Who would have believed it?
Grandma You're a triumph, my dear, a triumph!

The song picks up and this time is full of "go"

All   She'll be sweet to look at in
(*except*   The silk and satin,
Jenifer)   Delightful and demure

> She'll win every part of
> The glittering heart of
> The world of *haute couture.*

Jenifer   I'm Red, Red,
>   Red Ridinghood,
>   Goodbye tomboy
>   And Girl Guidinghood;
>   I'm the girl that nobody's going to ignore.
>   I'll be Red Ridinghood
>   For evermore.

A dance break follows around the new feminine Jenifer (hereafter referred to as "Red") with a very slow reprise from "I'm the girl that nobody's going to ignore"

Red Oh, how wonderful it feels, sort of light and airy.

Orme That girl needs a father.

Grandma Why? She's got me. We'll see you later everyone, at the fancy dress picnic outside the village, with sheep and maypoles.

Red Oh, what fun.

Harold A fancy dress picnic?

Grandma See to it, Alice, while we go and talk seriously about a lot of silliness.

Grandma and Red Ridinghood begin to sweep off

Hilda But what about the A Number One Wolf Trap from your great grandfather's time?

Red Oh, never mind about the wolf. He'll probably go away if you ignore him.

Red and Grandma leave, Grandma putting her tongue out at Hilda

Hilda She's abandoned us in the middle of Wolf Time.

Old Lemuel Which calls for a drop of the Old Dratted.

Hilda Put that away and you two get on duty. Greg and I will go and see if we can find the trap.

Alice Wait for me!

Alice, Hilda and Gregory leave

Old Lemuel and Winifred go on duty at the back with the Old Dratted

Thelma And I'll go and have a cry because she's all grown up, Roger.

Orme There's always need for a mother's guiding hand to love and argue with, my little pot of wisdom.

Thelma and Mr Orme leave

Winifred and Old Lemuel nod over the bottle

George and Harold creep on

George (*to the audience*) Did you see that cheeky little chubby chops in the red whatsit.

Harold (*to the audience*) Did you see her, did you?

George Used to look all gristly and tough?

Harold Edible as old wellingtons?

George Well, now we see she's just exactly the perfect size, don't we, Harold? Just exactly and precisely the perfect size.

Harold And nice, George.

George It's either her or us, Harold.

Harold It's her, George.

George Then nip off to the Wild and Windy Marshes with the news that a really first class main dish has been found while I work out what to give him for starters.

Harold Must I?

George If you want to keep your job.

Harold Right, I'm off.

George And tell him to be charming.

Harold goes

He can be charming, you know.

A faint wolf-howl is heard

When he isn't being impatient. No idea of self-control, wolves.

George creeps off, round the proscenium arch

Old Lemuel Did you hear that?

Winifred Oh, I did. And Jenifer isn't here.

Old Lemuel }
Winifrid } *together* Jenifer, Jenifer, the Wolf Trap!

Mr Orme enters with Hilda, Alice, Gregory and the Wolf Trap—a spectacular contraption

Orme Don't panic, my merry people, we've found it.

Old Lemuel Is that the A Number One Wolf Trap of old?

Orme It is and it works like this. (*He tries to work it, and fails*)

Alice I don't think it does, Mr Orme sir.

Old Lemuel (*to the audience*) I wonder if one or two of you young things could give us a hand with it, could you?

Hilda Good thinking, Lemuel.

Children come on stage and help with the Wolf Trap in various ways, catching Mr Orme and so on

Orme (*eventually*) No, no, no. What we need is strategy. You take this and this and we will hide and wait for someone to come on.

All move as instructed

George enters with a waiter's pad

All (*whispering*) A tweaker, a tweaker.

George I think we'll start with the soup, to calm him down a bit. Cold fish soup.

George has to be coaxed forward, with tricks, and is eventually caught

Old Lemuel Caught you, you wicked tweaker you.

George Let me out.

Orme Certainly not.

Hilda You're a tweaker, aren't you?

George What if I am?

Hilda Leave him there to starve.

George All right, all right, I am a tweaker and I will tell you a secret if you let me go.

Hilda What secret?

George About the Wolf.

Hilda Let him out.

George The secret is the Wolf is going away, he doesn't like it here. . . .

Harold Oh. (*To the audience*) Is he?

Audience NO!!

George takes the opportunity to escape

Hilda He's coming here? Get those children safely back to their seats and man the barricades.

Orme As manager of the bank——

Hilda And take that tweaker prisoner.

Orme He's gone!

Hilda You incompetent manager, find him! Find him all of you. Seek him here, seek him there, seek that Tweaker everywhere!

There is a frantic search, during which everyone including the children, leaves the stage

The Lights darken, wolf howls are heard . . .

SCENE 6

Mr Charles Grows Excited

The Wild and Windy Marshes

The Wolf is howling with delight. Harold is nervous

Wolf Tender, you say, and young, and served up in a red cloak?

Harold Exactly, Mr Charles.

The Wolf howls. There is thunder and lightning

And she's what you'd call beautiful as well.

Wolf Beautiful? Tell me, tell me.

Harold She's just beautiful, that's all. Some people are, some people aren't, and she is.

Wolf D'you think she might reach into an old wolf's heart, and understand me, being beautiful and so on?

Harold Well——

Wolf D'you think she'd say, "Who's a handsome shaggy old wolf, then, who's a poor lost lonely creature?"

Harold Well——

Wolf And, if I answered, "I am, I'm a poor lost lonely creature", do you think she'd say "Aaah"?

Harold Aaah?

Wolf Aaah. Aaah. Aaah. (*He makes the audience do it and then*) Silence! I don't want your pity. I'm splendid and strong like an oak tree. (*He howls*)

Thunder and lightning

Harold Yes, well, George said it would be all right if you were charming, Mr Charles.

Wolf I'm always charming! Look at me! Charming! And I'll show her I'm charming, and she must like me or I'll eat her, and I'll eat you, and I'll eat everybody because I'm charming! Look! charming, charming! (*He howls round the place*)

Harold Take it away! We don't want to see him any more! He's frightening the children.

The front cloth comes down

SCENE 7

Preparations For A Meal

In front of the cloth. Harold is sweating

George enters, pushing a trolley covered with a cloth

George Pleased, was he?

Harold I think so. You can't always tell.

George Well, the old groaners are getting a bit uppity, so we'll have to calm him down, or they'll catch him.

Harold How do we do that?

George Soup. We'll make him some soup.

Harold Oh, I like making soup. It reminds me of the old days when I really was in the feeding business.

George pulls the cloth off the trolley. There is a cooking pot, a chopping board, a goldfish bowl with fish in, a hamster cage, a mouse cage, and a box marked chicken. Also a large mallet

George There's the cooking pot, and for the basic flavour, what about a nice couple of goldfish?

Harold Oh, goldfish, lovely, get them out.

Business follows, then a fish is put onto the board and splattered with the mallet. The remains are popped into the bowl. Note:– not a real goldfish of course, but pieces of carrot

George Get the other one.

Business, as before, with the second goldfish

Harold It's delicate work, cooking for a gentleman.
George Takes skill, taste, cordon bleu.
Harold All of that. How about a bit of hamster to give piquancy?
George Get him out.

Harold hammers. The hamster is held up as flat stiff fur, and put into the pot

Harold Chicken, yes. (*He takes the cardboard box by a handle. It jerks about in his hand. There is a great squawking. He puts his hand in, and is bitten*) Ouch.
George Here, give it me. (*He puts the box on the ground and jumps on it several times, then from the flattened wreckage takes out a rubber plucked and trussed chicken which he puts into the pot*)
Harold That just leaves the mice.
George Oh, they're too good for Mr Charles. We'll have those.

George and Harold take the chocolate mice from the case, one each, and eat them. The tails are last and have to be sucked in like spaghetti

Harold I think some people down there think we're cruel and heartless.
George Do you? Cruel and heartless?
Harold Well, listen to this then.

Song 8: It's a Living

George ⎫
                together
Harold ⎭

It's a living,
It's a living,
We're just a pair of fellas making bread, my friends,
We're obeying
That old saying,
"If you haven't got a living you are dead, my friends."
So, our living,
Is a living,
And we just take whatever heaven sends, my friends,
Though our calling
Is appalling,
And one we cannot brag of to our friends, my friends.

We close our eyes and hope to make a bob or two,
And if you think it's heartless then consider, do,

There but for the rolling of the dice go you,
It's a difficult living, my friends.

Harold   It's a living,
Be forgiving,
We'd like to be two people you admire, my friends;

George   Like the others,
We had mothers,
We cuddled up beside them by the fire, my friends,

George ⎫ *together*   But it's funny,
Harold ⎭   Making money
Is now the only thing that we can do, my friends,
And our living,
Keeping living,
Is keeping us from being friends with you, my
friends,

We'd like to be two sweeties and know how it feels,
And live in love and harmony and all those deals,
For then we'd dedicate our lives to Meals on
Wheels,
It's a difficult living, my friends.

Harold And now to the picnic.
George The picnic with additional surprises.

George and Harold go

SCENE 8

The Picnic

A country scene, evening, around the Maypole

*Seated and drinking champagne are Old Lemuel, Mr Orme, Thelma, Winifred
and Red. On guard is Hilda with the blunderbuss. Two sheep are present.
Grandma is being hostess. All have a touch of fancy dress*

Grandma (*to the audience*) There you see, a nice civilized evening and not a
wolf to be seen.
Harold HA!
Winifred (*drunkenly*) 'Zactly.
Grandma And the sheep. Dear cuddly things. If only you were ten years
older and had fewer legs. Now, you are going to be our watch dogs. You
just go out there and bleat if you see a wolf, will you? Bleat? Ah. Aren't
they lovely? Off you go.

The sheep go

Winifred Now, Red Ridinghood, tell us how it feels in your new clothes.

Red Oh Winifred, it just feels truly, truly beautiful and scrumptious.

Grandma Of course it does.

Red Oh Gran!

Grandma Oh Red!

Old Lemuel Oh heavens.

Orme Lemuel?

Old Lemuel She's all stuck up.

Red I'm just truly, truly beautiful and scrumptious, that's all.

Grandma And you haven't seen a lot of that since I was young, have you? Mr Orme, move a little farther off, you know how I feel about your garter. Any Red Indians, Hilda?

Hilda (*indicating the audience*) They said the wolf——

Grandma The sheep will let us know if there's trouble, dear, baa, baa, baa, they'll warn us. Relax, or you'll break something.

Winifred I think it's time we did a dance round the Maypole.

Grandma Oh, yes! Which one shall we do?

Old Lemuel The one we invented when we killed the Wolf all those years ago.

Grandma (*sharply*) What?

Thelma Very good Lem, it'll scare him off if he's still about.

Grandma All right then, if we must.

Winifred Come along, Alice and Gregory. You can stop picking those daisies, now.

Hilda Winifred!

Grandma As I recall, Lemuel, this dance gets rather over-stimulating. I hope I'm up to it.

Old Lemuel I am if you are.

Greg and Alice come in

Song 9: Maypole Song

(*Singing*) Down in the hollow where the villagers play,
     Everyone's safe for the livelong day.
     We caught the Wolf who roamed all free,
     And tied him alive to the Maypole tree.

Chorus

     Boo to the wicked and boo to the bad,
     Boo to the worst friend you ever had,
     Boo to his roars and his horrible sneers,
     Boo to the cauliflowers in his ears.

     Tied him alive and tickled his toes,
     Watched how the tears dripped down his nose,
     Chopped off his tail with an awful din,
     And stuck it back on with a drawing pin.

Repeat chorus

> Tickled him here and tickled him there,
> Tickled that Wolf 'most everywhere,
> Tickled him pink, tickled him red,
> Tickled old Wolf till he dropped dead.

Repeat chorus

Grandma is overcome by the speed of the dance (music 9a)

Grandma Oh! Oh my goodness. Alice, my funny pills. I'm all of a glow.
Winifred Oh, Mrs Ridinghood Senior, have you overdone it?
Grandma All my life but it hasn't mattered up to now. Oh thank you dear.
Red Oh, Grandma, Grandma, what is it?
Grandma Nothing, nothing, my darling, I'll just go and have a lie down.
Red I'll come too.
Grandma No! You stay and enjoy the lovely evening and practise your curtseys like I meant you to.
Hilda Suppose the Wolf comes?
Grandma The sheep will bleat, Hilda, don't worry.
Winifred Come and guard the village, Hilda.
Grandma Just give me a hand all of you and then you can come back here and sober up. Come along, Thelma.
Hilda Oh—all right.

All exit, except for Red

Red So I'm alone with my daydreams, and also beautiful. Oh, I do like being lovely Red Ridinghood instead of scrawny Jenifer, building silly traps and things. I mean, it is nice having people say I'm—you know— pretty and everything. But I must practise my curtseys so they'll say it more. How do you do? (*She curtsies*)

Clouds and lighting are seen

> How do you do? (*She curtsies*)

Faint thunder is heard

> The Wolf appears, handsomely groomed and carrying a dead sheep. He imitates Red each time she curtsies

How do you do? (*She curtsies*). How do you do? (*She curties again*). How do you—— (*She turns suspiciously*)

Very loud thunder is heard. Lightning flashes

> Oh! Help! Help!

The Wolf cuts off her retreat

Wolf Sh, sh, sh. (*He approaches Red*) There, I'm just a handsome old thing, aren't I? And you're just a fluffy little red chicken.
Red No I'm not, I'm a rather difficult person, and you're a wicked and dangerous creature.

31

Wolf Oh don't be so provincial. I'm simply charming, aren't I? Charming, like you are.

Red What happened to that, then? (*She points to a sheep which is in two halves*)

Wolf It just broke in my hands.

Red Please don't make jokes.

Wolf Jokes?

Red You've come to eat me, haven't you?

Wolf Only if you make me. I've really come to be friends with you, because you're beautiful and you're kind and we're going to go for a walk together, aren't we?

Red No thank you very much.

Red (*restraining himself*) People do go for walks together when they like each other.

Red The trouble is I don't like you very much, I'm afraid.

Wolf You do.

Red I don't.

Wolf You do.

Red I don't.

Wolf You do, you do, you do! I'm charming and you like me and I'm going to eat you if you don't!

Red No. Please don't eat me, please. (*Indicating the sheep*) You've got that instead, if you're hungry.

Wolf (*throwing the sheep away*) Do you think you could understand me?

Red I could try.

Wolf I do tricks you know. Flowers. (*He produces some flowers*) Oranges. (*He produces oranges*) Hankies. (*He produces hankies*)

Red gasps each time he produces these things

Red Oh, they're pretty.

The Wolf produces several hankies and leads Red round the stage, giving them to her. Finally there is one he will not let go of

Red Please let me have it.

Wolf No. It's mine. Like you are.

Red I'm not yours.

Wolf Yes, you are!

Red No I'm not!

Wolf You are, I've given you presents and you're mine. (*He howls and chases after Red*)

Red escapes his clutches

Thelma (*off*) Red Ridinghood!

Red I am here! Get into safety! The Wolf is here!

Red exits

Hilda (*off*) I knew it! Stand clear while I shoot.

There are shouts off and the blunderbuss goes off

Thunder and lightning

Wolf Come back, come back! It's always the same with humans! They won't give in and be lovely. Well, I'll get revenge for this!! I'll eat you, you stupid little girl, I'll eat you, I'll never rest until I eat you!

Song 10: I Cry Revenge

(*Singing*) I cry revenge, revenge for all my people.
I will not rest, I will not dream or sleep.
I will lift high the name of our great wolfish kingdom,
The beast of beasts his destiny must keep.

Our noble line, unyielding without mercy
Will always love me, honouring my name,
Let humans know my steely heart and claws will conquer
And human blood through me will purge our shame.

I cry revenge, revenge for all my people.
I will not rest, I will not dream or sleep.
I will lift high the name of our great wolfish kingdom,
The beast of beasts his destiny must keep.

The Wolf exits at the end of the song

George and Harold enter

George Trouble Harold. We might've lost our living.
Harold Let's nip off and have, as it were, a think.
George And maybe an ice cream. It looks as though it might be the interval.

George and Harold exit through the audience

CURTAIN

ENTR'ACTE

George and Harold Lose A Living

George and Harold enter from the audience

Harold Let's get up there, George.
George Up into our private cosy little place.

They are now in front of the cloth

Now dear friends, we've had our ponder, and we have to say that things are in a pretty state.
George A dog's, as it might be, dinner.
Harold Because when Mr Charles blows his top like this, you don't know where you stand.

Lightning and thunder

The Wolf is revealed as in Act I, Prologue

Wolf I'll tell you where you stand. You stand on your own. Go! I've finished.
George
Harold } *together* Us. What about our living?
Wolf Go and find another living. From now on I don't need you.
George } *together* { What about your little morsels, rat paté and hedgehog
Harold } { fillets?
Wolf I don't want those! You know I don't want those. I'm waiting for Red Ridinghood.
George Red Ridinghood?
Harold She won't come to you just like that.
George You need our subtlety; our, as it might be, clever cunning.
Wolf Oh, she'll come, I know she'll come! I'm waiting for her in the heart of the forest by the Great Oak Tree. And you two, keep out of my way! Bunglers, keep out of my way.
George } *together* What does he mean, bunglers?
Harold }

Song 11: Wolf Rap

The Wolf begins rapping, starting with a refrain

Wolf (*singing*) The Great Oak, The Great Oak,
The Big Meal happens at the Great Oak.

Now I've been waiting my whole life through,
For a plateful juicy and spanking new,

That plate's now coming, and coming good,
With a brand new flavour called Ridinghood.

It's red and raw and sweet and young,
And one big swallow takes it over your tongue.

It fills you, thrills you, lip-smacking fine,
And every last crumb is mine, mine, mine.

At the Great Oak, the Great Oak.
When the big meal happens at the Great Oak.

Verse 2 is deliberately double the length of verse 1

I'm going to be eating all by myself,
And I don't want company, I don't want help.

I don't want watching as I swallow her down,
So you two take yourselves away to town.

By the lonesome, own some, one man tree,
I'll be eating my girl, just her and me,

And I don't want any interfering men like you
To come along a-telling me what to do.

He becomes increasingly mad

I can manage on my own, I'm a great big boy,
I can play by myself with my Ridinghood toy.

I'm charming and I'm handsome, and the best there is!
She'd better stop pretending she's a stuck-up Miss,
'Cos she knows where I am, and she knows where I stay,
And she feels very nearly the same darn way!
She can talk, she can walk, she can smile like a dream,
And when dinner time is on us she can scream, scream,
    scream!

At the Great Oak, the Great Oak.
When the big meal happens at the Great Oak.

At the end of the Wolf Rap the Wolf fades, lights return to normal

Harold Hey, come back!
George Scabby tail!
Harold Mouldy head!
George Fleas' delight!
Both Smelly breath!

George We're not bunglers!

Harold Oh—leave him, George. You have to admit that as an employer he was growing unreliable and nasty.

George But we've got no living, nowhere to cuddle down at night.

Harold We'll manage, George.

George We won't. We're going to wither away and die. Ahh!

The audience goes "Ahh". Harold encourages this, to make George feel better

Hilda and Mr Orme enter

Hilda Now, now, now. What's all this?

Harold My poor friend was saying that we're going to wither away and die.

Hilda Good.

George What?

Orme She said "good".

Hilda We're in charge now, Red Ridinghood is safe at home, and we don't want any tweakers, or friends of the Wolf, or anything like that.

Orme Yes, we're in charge now, especially me and we don't want any tweakers or——

Harold But we're not tweakers any more, kind sir.

George We've given up the Wolf, kind sir.

Harold We want to be on your side, now.

Hilda
Mr Orme } *together* Well you can't be. Go!

Harold We know something about the Wolf and what he's up to.

George Yes we do.

Harold And if you let us be on your side, we'll tell it to you.

Hilda Don't play games with us, young man. Get out.

Orme Suppose they do know something?

Hilda They don't. They're liars through and through.

George
Harold } Oh no we're not.

Orme
Hilda } Oh yes, you are.

Song 12: We Know Something

George **Harold** }	We know something you don't know!
Orme **Hilda** }	No you don't!
George **Harold** }	Yes we do. You'll be sorry soon, oho!
Orme **Hilda** }	Yaboo sucks to you!
George **Harold** }	We know plans and we know plots, We know horrors!

Orme **Hilda** }	We don't care!
George **Harold** }	We know lots and lots and lots, We shan't tell you, so there!
Chorus	
George **Harold** }	We know something!
Orme **Hilda** }	No you don't!
George **Harold** }	Yes we do!
Orme **Hilda** }	Nothing!
George **Harold** }	Something We're not telling you!
Orme **Hilda** }	You tell stories, you tell fibs!
George **Harold** }	No we don't!
Orme **Hilda** }	Yes you do Squeeze the juice from babies' bibs!
George **Harold** }	Well then, so do you.
Orme **Hilda** }	You've got warts upon your thumb.
George **Harold** }	You pick your noses.
Orme **Hilda** }	You eat scabs, You've got blackheads on your bum.
George **Harold** }	You've got legs like crabs.
Chorus	
George **Harold** }	We know something really grot.
Orme **Hilda** }	Turnip face!

George
Harold 〉 Bogey stew!

Orme
Hilda 〉 Don't you pong an awful lot,
Ugh and yukky pooh!

George
Harold 〉 You'll be sorry when you hear, much too late.

Orme
Hilda 〉 Smelly toes!

George
Harold 〉 You've got bees' wax in your ear,

Orme
Hilda 〉 And black stuff up your nose!

Chorus twice

Orme Cacky——
Hilda Beastly——
George Slimey——
Harold Greasy——
Orme Filthy——
George Lousy——
All Pooh!——

Grandma is heard shouting off, and the Cloth goes up on . . .

ACT II

SCENE 1

The Village, Evening

Grandma is present, carrying a walking stick, and with the rest of the villagers. Only Red Ridinghood is missing. Music continues under dialogue

Grandma Stop! What rambunctiousness is this?

Orme ⎱ *together* Lo! The frightful tweakers!
Hilda ⎰

George ⎱
       together, kneeling   No longer tweakers ma'am, but honest folk who'll tell you something useful if they can be on you side.
Harold ⎰

The music gets very "William Walton"

Grandma Friends! We must unite if we're to keep our village safe for youth and beauty to grow up in. All for one and one for all has always been my way of life, and now it is more so, with these dear trees, and this dear grass, and that dear village and most of all dear you, dear happy you, dear band of yokels all so threatened by that filthy toe rag of a wolf. Yes, join us, er——

George George.

Grandma ——and er——

Harold Harold.

Grandma I knew a Harold once, and he was a man of action, so let us fight for the joy of living and freedom from the Wolf!

Orme ⎱ *together* But they're tweakers!
Hilda ⎰

Music 12a: George and Harold Recitative

George *reciting* ⎱ Nay, hark! This plan to us the Wolf made clear——
Harold *together* ⎰ He's sure he will succeed in this endeavour-
To the Great Oak, he'll call your granddaughter dear,
And there, he'll swallow her for ever!

All Fiend! Fiend!
Thelma Oh!
Grandma But we'll frustrate him quite.
Friends of the forest, to save this girl, unite!

Song 13: Grandma's Call to Arms

(*Singing*)   Come from the cow shed,
Come from the stall,
Come from your humble cots,
To answer the call.
Leave off your bickering,
Surrender your pride,
Grandma is calling you,
So stand by her side.

All   Come from the farm yard,
Come from the hay,
Come from from whatever
You've been shovelling today.
Come from the church hall,
The institute, the pub,
Come from the revels of
The Working Men's Club.

Come from the hill side,
Come from the dale,
Come from the cabbages,
The sprouts and the kale.
Come from the corn stooks,
Thrill to the call,
All is for one of us and
One is for all!

Grandma We must double the guards at each end of the village and lay plans for secret raids into the forest. We must learn how to swing from branches and jump out of trees without being seen. We must learn how to punch and hit and smash—Aaaaaaaaaaaaaaaaaah! OOoooooooo! (*She continues moaning*)

Winifred Oh, Mrs Ridinghood Senior!

Alice Ma'am, ma'am, ma'am!

Old Lemuel My sainted aunt, what is it?

Hilda (*to George and Harold*) Who did that? Did you do that?

George ⎱ *together* No!
Harold ⎰

Hilda You're trying to stop us just when we are getting going.

George ⎱ *together* No!
Harold ⎰

Gregory I'll deal with you, I'll show you.

Hilda Stay where you are, Gregory!

Grandma It's another of my twinges. Give me my twinge pills, Alice. (*She sinks onto the village seat*)

Winifred The twinge pills.

Alice Oh, we haven't any, ma'am, they're at home.

Grandma One of my funny pills, then.

Alice Oh, oh, oh Mrs Ridinghood Senior, you've had them all.

Grandma All!

Alice Yes, all, all, they're all gone and oh, you're going to die and it's all going to be my fault, oh, foolish little person that I am!

Grandma Alice stop it! I'm not going to die—Aaaaaaaah, ooooooh, my leg.

Orme I'll rub it for you.

Grandma Undo my corset someone.

Winifred Here on the village green?

Grandma Afraid of riots, Winifred?

Alice Oh! And my poor little fingers are frozen in the cold night air. I can't do it! Oh I'm so hopeless, hopeless, hopeless. Gregory will never marry me.

Gregory I will.

Alice No.

Hilda Lem, corset.

Lem goes to it with a sort of "Aha!"

Winifred You two look the other way.

George With pleasure.

Grandma You don't know what you're missing.

Gregory Not much, I've seen it.

Grandma is now in an undignified posture owing to various massagings and undoings

Hilda This is a great upset. Have you no pills at all, Alice?

Alice We've just a few at home, Hilda, but I never did the shopping, ma'am, because of all that happened. Oh ma'am, I am a stupid girl, oh I am a useless maid, a silly servant not worthy of the parlour. (*She wails*)

Grandma Alice give over! It's me that's in pain—aaaaaah!

Thelma What are you doing Roger?

Orme Helping your mother.

Thelma I'll do that.

Grandma is being shaken by Old Lemuel trying to loosen her stays

Alice Careful, she's delicate.

Grandma What is it, Lem?

Old Lemuel I've got my finger caught! (*In the corset, he means*)

Hilda Heave, go on heave.

Grandma Ahhhh ahhhhh!

Old Lemuel (*his finger now free*) Aaaah, that's better.

Hilda The question is what are we going to do?

Miles of corsets come away. Grandma moans. Her fine dress collapses and she has to hold it up

Winifred (*helping to reel in the corsets*) She'll catch her death of cold without her corsets on the village green in the evening of the autumn, she will, Alice.

Grandma Then get me home.

All activity ceases

Hilda I knew it, you've let us down. First the picnic and now this.

Grandma I haven't let you down. You can manage quite well on your own so I want to go to my bed in my own home.

Hilda What about this "all for one and one for all" talk? Grandma calls so come and stand beside her.

Grandma Well I'm pooped, Hilda, pipped at the post and pooped. So you and Mr Orme will have to take over. You always wanted to be in charge, anyway.

Hilda Right. Which of you will take her back to her own cottage?

Orme You'll be quite safe if you take the long way round by the big broad path.

Old Lemuel Wolves never go there.

Hilda Which one?

Orme Which one? Come along. Who will volunteer?

Alice We will, Greg will. Greg's brave.

Sheepish looks all round

Red Ridinghood enters

Red I'll take you, Grandma.

Grandma What?

All (*variations of*) No! Certainly not! You of all people, no. That girl needs a father, (*etc.*)

Red We'll be quite safe if we go the long way by the big broad path. As Lemuel says, wolves never go there.

Harold But the Wolf is waiting for you by the Great Oak in the heart of the forest.

Grandma You come tomorrow, my love, when it's daylight and bring me a nice basket of goodies with all my favourite medicines.

Red I want to go now.

Grandma Well, you can't.

Thelma }
Orme } *together* No, you can't.

Red (*fiercely*) But I want to, I want to!

Hilda No.

Harold (*interrupting Red*) Red Ridinghood, come here!

Thelma Heh.

Harold (*to Red*) You're what I call a very nice young lady and a nice young lady can't go out there, into that wood, at this time of night, dressed all in smarty boots red, with a hungry wolf waiting for her by the Great Oak in the heart of the forest sharpening his teeth. That is not, truly it is not, as it were, sensible.

Red He's got a hanky he wouldn't give me.
Harold Forget that.
Red And it's exciting.
Harold It's too exciting. (*To the others*) Now instead of you, George and I will take Grandma through the forest tonight.
George Us?
Harold Yes, George. And tomorrow she can take Grandma a lovely basket of goodies through the safe daylight with your friends.
Grandma Oh yes, and you can bring all my favourite herbs and remedies to keep me young and beautiful and well regulated. Like a lady should be.
Harold So settle down and make a list.

Harold gives Red a pencil and sits her down as music for Song 14 begins

Thelma Is he in charge, Roger?
Orme He seems to be.
Hilda For the moment, but really it's me.
Orme It's me.
Grandma There's snap to that garter, I know.

Song 14: A Basket of Goodies

Harold (*singing*)   You'll bring a basket of goodies tomorrow,
                                          Take it along in the light of the dawn,
                                          Working to get it will lessen your sorrow,
                                          Here is a list of the things for the morn.

Grandma   Catmint and houseleek for cramps in the bones,
                                          Coltsfoot and comfrey for coughing, with rue.

Winifred   Samphire and gromel for gravel and stoneses,

Old Lemuel ⎫
Thelma   ⎬ *together*   Quince seed and pimpernel, hair to renew.

The song is then divided for voices

  Alice exits

                                          Costmary, Sanicle, Old Lady's Thistle,
                                          A spot of Monk's Rhubarb, all for the blood,
                                          Knapweed and Ditchwort for wetting your whistle,
                                          For baths, Lady's Bedstraw, and lashings of mud.

                                          Butterbur, Hawthorne for pains after shopping,
                                          Devil's Bit, Margold, soothing for bumps,
                                          Stonecrop and Figwort for stopping the popping,
                                          Clivers for fatness and Cudweed for mumps.

                                          Celandine cures a disease I won't mention,
                                          Herb Robert too, they will help you to sit.

> Sweet Ciceley, Tamarisk, both ease the tension
> Kidneywort, Horsetail for flushing you fit.
>
> Add for arthritis some Old Agrimony,
> Burdock and Camomile, all for the pot,
> Hawkwood and Horehound, and Holly and Honey
> Wintergreen, Marsh Mallow, Bugloss, the lot.
>
> You'll bring a basket of goodies tomorrow,
> Take it along in the light of the dawn,
> Working to get it will lessen her sorrow,
> Those are the things she will bring in the morn.

Grandma leans towards Harold, near to George

Grandma Goodbye! Goodbye! See you tomorrow Red Ridinghood. I think I need to lean on you, Harold.

Harold Guard her well, everyone. She's very precious.

Grandma (*to the helpful George*) I said Harold. Now we shall have to stay very close together in the wood to keep our spirits up. I feel better already.

George, Harold, Grandma and Gregory go, Grandma looking rather bedraggled but gazing at Harold

Orme Well then, for the rest of us it's bedtime, I think.

Red Bedtime?

Orme We'll have to be up early to get the basket filled. Come along.

Old Lemuel Come along, Red Ridinghood. You don't want to be swallowed down by that horrid old Wolf.

Red Oh—all right then.

Gregory and Alice enter. Alice has a basket with some herbs in it

Alice There, I'm not so silly, am I? I got a basket and I half filled it with goodies already and there'll only be a little bit to do in the morning and I'll leave it on the seat so we'll remember it.

Gregory Alice, you're a wonder.

Alice Well I am, aren't I?

Gregory Well, you are.

Gregory and Alice rub noses

All exit, except for Red

Red (*gazing at the basket*) D'you know, Grandma really needs that basket now, because it's got all her medicines in it. (*She picks it up*) It would honestly be best if I took it to her straight away because these medicines might be the very ones she needs tonight, mightn't they? I won't go near the Great Oak. I won't. Even though he still has a handkerchief he won't give me. I'll go slowly by the big broad path to give Grandma time to get home, because I'm being an awfully thoughtful and kind girl. That's why I'm doing this, I won't go near the Great Oak at all. I'll just wander off along the big broad path.

Red exits

Thelma (*off*) Come on now, Red Ridinghood.

Thelma enters

It's time for cocoa. Red Ridinghood? She's gone! Red Ridinghood's gone!

Mr Orme enters

Orme What?

Old Lemuel enters

Old Lemuel What?

Winifred enters

Winifred Oh she has. And the goodies—She's taken the goodies.

Thelma screams

Alice enters

Alice Oh, it's all my fault, I'm foolish all over again, I am, I am.
Gregory Now, Alice.
Orme Who was in charge of her? Who was looking after her? Who was on sentry duty?

Hilda enters and steps forward

Hilda (*indicating the front cloth*) Bring that thing down will you, quickly. Quickly!

The cloth comes in and Hilda steps forward leaving the others behind

Orme (*behind the cloth*) But I'm in charge!

SCENE 2

Crisis Plans

In front of the cloth

Hilda (*to the audience*) Right. There's been a blunder, I'm afraid. Cold autumn evening, Grandma croaking in her cottage, Wolf waiting by the Great Oak to swallow Red Ridinghood, and Red Ridinghood—extremely foolishly—gone off on her own with the basket of goodies to cheer the old lady up without telling anyone. Suddenly, everything's gone wrong. (*She looks offstage*) Anyone got any ideas?

Thelma enters

No, no, Thelma, not you.

Mr Orme enters

Orme My little Boadicea, you aren't built for this sort of thing. Hilda, I'm in charge.

Thelma It's my family that's in danger and I've had an idea. (*She indicates the audience*) They can help us.

Orme No, no, it's much too dangerous.

Thelma I bet they don't think so, do you? No, you see, all of them difficult, just like Jenifer. Now, here's my idea. When you see the Wolf coming, you shout to us. Mr Orme, you go off and come on as the Wolf and we'll go off there and come on when they shout.

Hilda But Thelma——

Thelma Sh!

Business of getting the audience to shout a warning of the Wolf

That's very good. Then you see, when we hear that we'll be able to run on and do something splendid. All right, Hilda.

Hilda Very well done, Thelma, and quite surprising. But what I meant was, we need——

Thelma Lanterns, and woolly hats, and scarves and coats because it's cold. Can you bring on coats and scarves and lanterns?——

The others—Gregory, Winifred, Old Lemuel and Alice—come on with the required properties

Orme And pitch forks and blunderbusses and things like that.

Hilda Yes, but the thing is——

Orme And the Wolf Trap, we need that.

Thelma No, we don't want the Wolf Trap.

Gregory Too complicated.

Winifred All we need is ourselves, Mr Orme, our brave little selves.

Alice And our stupid little selves too.

Hilda Some of us have got those, all right.

Orme Right then, off we go.

Hilda And that's my point. Where do we go to? Grandma's? By the long way, along the big broad path?

Old Lemuel (*wisely*) No, we go to the Great Oak 'cos that's where the danger is. And Red Ridinghood will go there because it's exciting.

Winifred It's very frightening.

Orme Yes it is.

Hilda What if it is?

Alice That's where we have to begin.

Orme Light the lanterns. It's going to be cold and dark among all those trees.

Gregory Ooooohh.

Hilda Don't worry. I'm in charge, Gregory.

They all go

SCENE 3

At the Great Oak

The Great Oak in the heart of the forest. It is moonlight. The Great Oak is the most noticeable tree but there is at least one other, and this is a movable one, at the moment containing the Wolf

The scene really begins in the previous scene for all the actors simply walk into the forest from where they stood before. They sing the following song, having acquired overcoats etc.

They are joined by Gregory, Alice, Old Lemuel and Winifred

Song 15: The Lantern Carol

All (*singing*) The frost is on our lanterns,
They glitter through the cold,
The brightest fires in all the wood,
Our lanterns make us bold.
The frost it cannot freeze them,
They bravely shed their light,
Dear lanterns always burn for us,
And keep away the night.

Hilda Here we are then, by the Great Oak in the heart of the forest.
Orme Sh!
All Sh! Sh! Sh!
Orme Now you Alice and Greg, you stay here in a group with Lem and watch who comes.
Alice Oh yes, Mr Orme. Greg's so brave.
Gregory Alice.
Orme And the rest of us will just have a quick creep round here, looking for tracks.
Thelma Whose?
Orme Anyone's. Come along, my little Indian hunter.
Hilda I thought I was in charge.
Orme I think you'll find it's my turn.

Hilda, Winifred, Mr Orme and Thelma go

Old Lemuel That's it, and as it's very cold, we'll all have a drink of the Old Dratted while we wait to see if Red Ridinghood turns off the big broad path because of her curiosity.
Alice She never will.

Lem takes out some cups (old and chipped) and pours everyone a drink, and hands them round

Old Lemuel She will. I bet she will. (*He moves off*) I'll just—er—call of nature.

Old Lemuel is hit by the furry arm of the Wolf from inside the tree. No one sees his demise. Old Lemuel falls behind the Great Oak

Alice Look over there, there's something moving.
Gregory No, there's nothing moving.
Alice I think there is. Lem! Lem! Lem, where are you? Lem, don't try to be funny.
Gregory I'll have a look for him. He might've seen Red Ridinghood.

Alice goes to one side of the stage and calls things like "Come to Alice, Lem"

Gregory goes near the Great Oak and calls. He gets distracted by furry thing One, a glove puppet, which causes him to come within striking distance of the furry arm. He is hit and falls out of sight behind the Great Oak

Alice He's not here, Greg. Greg? Greg! Oh Greg, my brave Greg, oh I'm a poor lost thing, help, help, help!

Furry thing Two, also a glove puppet, pops out of the Great Oak and whistles at Alice. She goes to it

Are you trying to tell me something? What? Speak up?

Alice listens very closely and gets bonked. She, too falls behind the Great Oak

Mr Orme, Hilda and Thelma enter

Orme There are no signs of anyone out there.
Thelma There are no signs of anything in here either.
Winifred Where've they gone?

Thunder and lightning

Wolf (*from his hiding place*) I've taken them away into the forest, out of the way. (*He laughs*)
Winifred Oh dear, Hilda, I don't think I feel quite as brave as I did.
Orme (*in a loud whisper*) I'm still in charge. And his voice came from over there. Come.

Mr Orme, Hilda, Winifred and Thelma, creep off after the voice

Thelma (*as they go*) You are impressive Roger.
Orme It's the training at head office.

The Wolf appears from the other side. Smiles at the audience, who shout.

The Wolf disappears

The Villagers rush on

Villagers Where? Where?
Audience There!

The Villagers rush off after the Wolf

Winifred, seeing a large butterfly, stays alone

Winifred Oh it's lovely. Oh I've never seen such a big butter-butter-butterfly—Ow!

Winifred is captured by the Wolf and led off

Hilda returns alone

Hilda Winifred? Winifred? Where are you?

The audience shouts

What? I can't get it clear.

A long butterfly net comes on, and Hilda is pulled off shouting

Mr Orme, Mr Orme! You're in charge now! Mr Orme. Ow!

Thelma and Mr Orme come on nervously

Orme That was Hilda! Things are bad if he's got Hilda.
Thelma Roger, these may be our last minutes together.
Orme They may be.
Thelma Then what I want to say is, I've been an awfully feeble mother, but I do love my daughter, and I do love you.
Orme Shall we sing, Thelma?
Thelma Yes, let's!

A furry thing goes whistling up a tree

Oh! There is a very funny furry thing there which might lead me to Red Ridinghood, so wait till I get back.
Orme Don't be silly.

The thing whistles down a tree

Thelma I am not being silly.

Thelma is drawn further and further after the thing which whistles up and down trees that lead further and further away

Orme Come here, do as you're told.
Thelma I've started making up my own mind.
Orme Well you're doing it wrong!
Thelma Don't be like that, Roger, it's lovely. Ow!

Thelma goes

Orme Oh, heavens, I'm alone. It's up to me to save the day. Well, I'm a bank manager and bank managers never give in.

The Wolf, badly disguised as a sheep, comes on at the back

Wolf Help, help, I'm a little lost sheep.
Orme I don't believe you.
Wolf Typical of a bank manager. Come on, I'm lost. (*He exits*).
Orme Are you? All right, I'll come and help. But I bet you turn out to be a wolf in sheep's clothing. Oldest trick in the book.

Mr Orme goes

Orme (*off*) I knew it! Ow!

Red Ridinghood enters

Red I know I said I wouldn't come here, and I did nearly get to Grandma's, but then I thought well, it is sort of exciting over there at the Great Oak— you know how it is——

A low laugh is heard, and the Wolf enters

Wolf I knew you liked me.
Red I hate you actually. I think you're mean and horrible.

Wolf Then why did you come?
Red I don't know.
Wolf I am marvellously handsome.
Red Well—I just thought—there was that handkerchief you haven't given
me—But perhaps after all I'll go. I've got to take this basket of goodies to
Grandma's house and——

The Wolf blocks Red Ridinghood's retreat

Wolf We're all alone. I only really enjoy my food when I'm alone. And
you're going to be the best food I've ever had.
Red I don't want to be food. I really don't want to be food.

Offstage, George and Harold sing "It's a Living". The Wolf turns

Wolf What are they doing here? The bunglers, spoiling everything, just
when I'm at my wonderfully amazing and relaxed best.
Red Help! Help! Come here!
Wolf Sh! Sh!
Red You won't enjoy eating me in front of them, will you.
Wolf No, it's all going wrong!
Red So goodbye, Mr Charles, and I don't ever want to see you again.

Red Ridinghood runs off

The Wolf, confused, howls

Wolf (*to the audience*) Oh be quiet! I don't interrupt you when you're
eating, do I? Grandma's house. That's where she said she was going and I
know a very short cut to that little place.

The Wolf dashes off

The Lights flicker

George and Harold run on

George } *together* Who is it. Who's there?
Harold
Harold Wolfie?
George Red Ridinghood?
Harold (*to the audience*) Has anyone been here?

The answer comes

George (*picking up the whistle*) I wonder whose this is? (*He blows it*)
Orme (*off*) Hello!
Harold Mr Orme?
Orme Yes.
Harold Come to the front where it's safe. Come and join Harold Hood and
his Merry Man! Bring that cosy cloth down will you?

The Front Cloth comes down

SCENE 4

Rallying Again

In front of the Cloth

Harold and George have the whistle

Orme (*off*) Where are you?
Harold Here at the front where it's safe.

George blows the whistle again

   Mr Orme enters

Orme I recognised that. Property of the bank.
Harold Where's everyone else?
Orme Oh, they're all over the place. No discipline, no self control, eaten by now, I shouldn't wonder.
George Even Hilda?
Harold Even Thelma?
Orme Oh Thelma, my little pâté de foie gras. We must do something, we must.
Harold Keep calm, keep calm.
George Just keep your head. I know what to do.
Harold And so do I.
George We'll get everyone together and then we'll all go and hunt for her.
Harold And we'll do it with Grandma's Call to Arms song.

A Song Sheet is lowered with one verse of Song 13 on it

George Ah, the, as it might be, Song Sheet.

George and Harold sing the song, with the help of the audience

   Alice and Gregory return

Alice Oh—oh Greg was so brave, and I was so frightened and it was all so lovely and hasn't it turned out nice.
Gregory Alice.
Orme Have you seen the others?
Gregory No.
Harold Right then. We'll sing it again, and *loudly*, to guide them to the stage.

The song is sung again

   Hilda and Winifred appear

Winifred Well, he was a real gentleman, even if he was a wolf, Hilda.
Hilda Rubbish.
Winifred Oh, he was.
Orme Where's Thelma?
Hilda Moaning away somewhere, I expect.
Winifred Oh, Hilda.

Hilda And Lem, drinking himself to death as usual.

The song is sung again

Thelma appears

Orme Oh my precious wood nymph, my own true sparrow of the forest.

Thelma Oh Mr Orme it was terrible, terrible. (*She dissolves into a high pitched weep*)

Gregory We just need Lem now.

Old Lemuel appears

Improvisation and song as they all return to the stage

Old Lemuel Oh that's better. Didn't like that tree, though it was fun up there.

George Now we're all together——

Harold ⎫

George ⎭ *together* Where's Red Ridinghood?

Harold (*to the audience*) Do you kind people know?

The audience indicates that Red is at Grandma's

Oh, Grandma's. That's where we'll go then.

George All the way back there?

Harold Line up.

Hilda I'm in charge.

Orme I'm in charge.

Harold By the left, quick march.

George My feet are killing me, Harold.

All march off

SCENE 5

Grandma's cottage, mainly furnished with a bed

Grandma is dressed for bed, as in Act I

Grandma There's nowhere like your own home when you're feeling poorly, is there? You can have a nice scratch and no-one can see. And it doesn't matter if you snore. No, I won't lock the door because Red Ridinghood might come before I wake up in the morning. (*She goes to sit on the bed*) I'll leave the bobbin on the latch and then she can get it and I won't have to clamber out of my dreams to see to it. Oh, I am looking forward to my dreams. I have this lovely one where I'm eighteen again, and working for two ugly sisters and there comes this invitation to the castle—— (*she is nearly in bed now*)

Wolf (*off, disguising his voice*) Grandma! Hello!

Grandma Red Ridinghood. The bobbin's on the latch dear, so just come in quickly, to be safe. (*She has her back to the door*) What ever are you doing coming through the wood at this time? I told you very strictly not to and those two nice waiters—(*she turns to see it is the Wolf*) Aaaaah! You're a wolf!

Wolf Yes.

Grandma I can tell by the wet nose and the nasty complexion. Will you come back tomorrow, please, because I'm not dressed for visitors.

Wolf No. I'm going to eat you, Mrs Ridinghood Senior.

The Wolf chases Grandma round the bed. Business, ending with him clouting her one unexpectedly. He listens to her heart and then lugs her into a laundry basket, saying—

There, I'll keep her for dessert. I don't want to spoil the taste of the little lady. Oh, I'll need these. (*He collects Grandma's shawl and cap and puts them on*) Now I am ready for Red Ridinghood (*He gets into bed but is instantly alert when Red Ridinghood is heard outside*)

Red (*off*) Hello! Grandma, are you awake?

Wolf Oh, Red Ridinghood. What are you doing here? The bobbin's on the latch so come in quickly, to be safe.

Red Ridinghood enters

Red Oh thank goodness. I just had to bring you this basket of goodies even though it wasn't quite ready.

Wolf How brave of you.

Red Yes, it was. I am afraid of the Wolf after all. He's horrid and cruel and . . . Grandma, your voice is funny.

Wolf I'm very frail, now.

Red And what big ears you have.

Wolf All the better to hear you with.

Red And what big eyes you have.

Wolf All the better to see you with.

Red And Grandma, what big teeth you have.

Red All the better to EAT YOU WITH!

Thunder, lightning, and screams are heard, all giving way to squelching

Black-out

SCENE 6

The Interior of the Wolf's Stomach

Red Ridinghood falls into it

Red (*screaming*) Oh! Oh! How horrible! Ugh! Let me out! Let—me—out!

Grandma falls into it also

Grandma Oh! Ooops! What a very unpleasant place.

Red Gran? Has he eaten you, too?

Grandma Yes dear, for pudding.

Red Oh Gran, this is awful, really awful.

Grandma I'm afraid it is, dear, and it's all my fault. I should've hunted that horrid Wolf with the rest of you and I shouldn't 've dressed you up in that saucy red outfit—I knew it, even then.

Red And I should've stopped at home tonight and I knew that as well. I can tell you though, I'm never going to speak to a wolf again as long as I live.

Grandma Very likely. We're being digested. That's what this treacly stuff does round our feet. It's taking the fur off my slippers.

Red Ugh. Can't we make him sick? This feels like his liver. (*She bounces*) Hey, be sick, go on, be sick.

Grandma (*joining in*) Go on, be sick.

Red It's no good. He's too fast asleep. If only we'd been just a tiny bit more sensible.

Grandma If we get out of here alive, that's what we'll be. A tiny bit more sensible.

Song 16: I Blame Myself

Red	If only I'd admitted he was beastly And seen through his terrible game
Grandma	If only I hadn't been a giddy young girl When I should've been a wise old dame.
Red	If only I hadn't been a bighead And the dress hadn't looked so smart.
Red **Grandma** }	If only, oh, if only We could just go again from the start.
Chorus	I blame myself for this terrible pickle I blame myself for this terrible mess It's all my fault, I must confess We've been particularly fickle, and I blame myself.
Red	If only I'd known that I'd be frightened Like I am in the middle of the night, When the stairs all creak in a spooky sort of way And there isn't any landing light.
Grandma	If only I hadn't tried to force you But had loved you with all of my heart—
Red **Grandma**	If only, oh if only We could just go again from the start.

Chorus

The music continues

Red (*sobbing on Grandma's shoulder*) Oh, Gran, Gran, I don't want this to happen.

Grandma No, dear, no. (*Calling*) Let us out! We're both too young and beautiful to die.

Both cry for help several times

Orme (*off*) There he is! Look!

Gregory (*off*) What a whopper. Careful, Alice.

Alice (*off*) Oh, the beast, the beast.

Grandma It's them! Hello! Hello!

Red We're in here everyone! Let us out quick.

Red
Grandma } *together* { We know where we went wrong now,
And we love life with all of our heart,
If only, oh if only,
We can just go again from the start.

Chorus

SCENE 7

Jenifer's Revenge

Grandma's cottage

The Villagers are round the bed—The Wolf is asleep

Gregory He's asleep, Alice.

Old Lemuel Then we're too late.

George
Harold } *together* He's, as it were, full.

Hilda With Grandma and Red Ridinghood.

Thelma Oh! The whole family in one gulp! Oh Roger!

Orme I know how you feel, little orphan, but at least we can get married now without objection.

Winifred It always does to look on the bright side, Thelma.

Old Lemuel Don't despair. We shall see what we shall see. (*He takes out a horn and shouts down it*) Hello in there. (*He listens through it*)

Red
Grandma } *together off* Hello out there.

Old Lemuel They're alive! Get me some scissors to cut him open with.

Thelma Oh! Thank goodness!

Harold Scissors, scissors, quick, George.

George Large scissors for cutting open wolves. (*He produces a huge pair of scissors*)

Old Lemuel Needle and thread.

Harold Needle and thread.

Old Lemuel Now let's see what's what.

George I would've been a surgeon if I'd had the Latin.

Gregory I can't stand the sight of blood.

Winifred Up with the sheet, Hilda.

Hilda I've got a certificate for First Aid. Ooh, Winifred!

Hilda and Winifred hold up a sheet to hide the operation

Old Lemuel Stand back. There we are and who's coming out of that horrid old wolf?

Grandma enters from behind the sheet

Grandma Oh Lem, I never thought I'd be so glad to see you. And even you, Mr Orme.

Red Ridinghood also enters

Red Thank you, Lem.

Thelma Oh Jenifer I am so glad to see you!

Red And I am glad to see you, Mother.

Grandma Oh! How strange!

Red Well I am——

Thelma So there——

Gregory Are you going to sew him up?

Red Wait, we've a score to settle with him haven't we, Gran.

Grandma A score dear?

Red (*to the audience*) What nasty things shall we put in his tummy that won't dissolve?

Grandma Epsom salts wouldn't go amiss, I can tell you.

Red Stones? Logs?

Red leads on the audience to suggest all sorts of things, even to things out of the audience, chairs from the boxes and so on. The Wolf is then sewn up

Red Now let's wake him up and see what he says.

Old Lemuel Wait a minute. There's one more thing yet. Get me a funnel. The Old Dratted. (*He chuckles, and pours Old Dratted down the Wolf's throat, then gives the bottle to Winifred*)

Gregory Ah. I know. There's one more thing. (*He gets a sparkler and puts it in the Wolf's mouth*)

Red Oh! And there's one more thing that will send him off with a real bang. (*She lights the sparkler*)

Hilda Quick, let's get that bed out of here.

All Yes, yes! (*etc.*)

They start pushing the bed offstage. Just as the bed leaves the stage the Wolf opens his eyes and sees the sparkler

The Wolf is pushed offstage

There is a loud bang. Some of the things put in the Wolf's stomach come back on stage

Grandma (*with a garden gnome or similar*)
Typical. You can never get rid of some things.

Red But we did get rid of the Wolf, absolutely and finally. And I can tell you, there are going to be no more wolves in *my* life. Never, never, never, never!

Grandma Don't stand like that dear, it isn't lady-like.

Red I'm never going to be lady-like again Grandma. I'm going to be a proper person who lives life to the full without getting eaten.

Grandma Oh well, suit yourself.

Thelma And Roger and I are going to live life to the full, aren't we, Roger?

Orme Yes, my little fireball.

Grandma Are you trying to tell me your garter has started to snap, Mr Orme?

Orme Ferociously.

Alice Oh and so has Gregory's ma'am—and we're getting married.

Gregory And you'll have to give her a rise so she can support me ...

Winifred And I'm just finishing the last drop of the Old Dratted that Lem gave me.

Old Lemuel (*dropping on his knees by Hilda*) And Hilda, I've long nourished a hopeless passion for you which——

Hilda No, thank you Lem. I've had my eye on this gentleman ever since he first tweaked me.

George Oh! Mr Charles! Mr Charles!

Hilda Come here! (*She grabs at George*)

Old Lemuel In that case Winifred, I have also long nourished a secret passion for which——

Winifred (*a little plastered*) Oh Lem, you are a one! (*She giggles*)

Old Lemuel But I'd rather be two, Winifred.

Winifred is helpless with laughter

Grandma (*hopefully*) So what about you, Harold? Have you any plans?

Harold I'm going to open a little vegetarian restaurant in the village, *Chez Harold*.

Grandma Oh, I can't go into trade at my age. I'll travel round the world and do good.

Hilda Good?

Grandma And why not? I'll try anything once.

Red So that's that, I've got a mother and father and we've learnt by our mistakes, haven't we, Gran?

Thelma Yes.

Red And if any of you see another wolf wherever you may be, just remember how we defeated ours, and how pleased we were when we'd done it.

Song 17: Maypole Song (Reprise)

All (*singing*)   Down in the hollow where the villagers play,
Everyone's safe for the livelong day,
They've caught the old Wolf who roamed all free,
And tied him alive to the Maypole Tree.

Boo to the wicked and boo to the bad,
Boo to the worst fright you ever had,
Boo to his roars and his horrible sneers,
Boo to the cauliflowers in his ears.

Tied him alive and tickled his toes,
Watched how the tears dripped down his nose,
Chopped off his tail with an awful din,
And stuck it back on with a drawing pin.

Chorus

CURTAIN

FURNITURE AND PROPERTY LIST

Only essential properties etc. are listed here. Further dressing may be added at the director's discretion.

PROLOGUE

Gauze (or other means of concealing Wolf)

ACT I

SCENE 1

On stage: Village green set, including a seat and trees

Off stage: Ladder, hammer and nails and bunting **(Jenifer** and **Thelma)**
List **(George)**
Revolver **(Mr Orme)**
Red Cross Box **(Winifred)**
Weapons **(Villagers)**

Personal: **All dancers:** Morris dancing equipment
Old Lemuel: bottle of "Old Dratted" (throughout)
Mr Orme: watch chain (throughout), whistle, bottle of pills

SCENE 2

On stage: Wild and Windy Marshes set

Off stage: Cut-out silhouettes of wolves with illuminated yellow eyes **(Stage Management)**

SCENE 3

On stage: Cottage set, interior or exterior
Housecoat

Off stage: Grandma's clothes **(Alice)**
Dog cart

SCENE 4

Frontcloth

SCENE 5

On stage: Village set, barricades, notices

Off stage: Present: *In it:* Red Ridinghood costume **(Alice)**

Mirror on wheels, covered by a large cloth **(Alice)**
Wolf Trap **(Mr Orme)**
Waiter's pad **(George)**

Personal: **Mr Orme:** revolver
Thelma: whistle
Grandma: handkerchief

SCENE 6

On stage: Wild and Windy Marshes set

SCENE 7

Frontcloth

Off stage: Trolley. *On it:* cooking pot, chopping board, goldfish bowl with a goldfish made from carrots. Hamster cage: *in it:* a flat piece of fur. Mouse cage: *in it:* two chocolate mice. Box marked "chicken" containing rubber chicken, plucked and trussed. Large mallet. All covered with a cloth **(George)**

SCENE 8

On stage: Country set, including maypole
Table. *On it:* glasses, a bottle of champagne
Chairs
Sheep

Off stage: Sheep, one split in half **(Wolf)**

Personal: **Hilda:** blunderbuss
Wolf: flowers, oranges, a number of large handkerchiefs

ENTR'ACTE

Gauze (as in Prologue)

ACT II

SCENE 1

On stage: Village set, seat and trees

Off stage: Basket with herbs **(Alice)**

Personal: **Grandma:** walking stick, removable corsets
Harold: pencil and paper

SCENE 2

Frontcloth

Off stage: Overcoats, lanterns **(all)**

SCENE 3

On stage: Great Oak
            Other trees
            Moveable tree
            Whistle

Off stage: Butterfly and butterfly net **(Stage Management)**
            Furry Thing **(Stage Management)**
            Sheep disguise **(Wolf)**
            Basket **(Red Ridinghood)**

Personal: **Old Lemuel:** cups
            Wolf: two furry glove puppets

SCENE 4

Frontcloth

Off stage: Song sheet **(Stage Management)**

SCENE 5

On stage: Cottage set, interior
            Bed on wheels. *On it:* a sheet for masking "operation"
            Laundry basket
            Shawl and cap

SCENE 6

On stage: Set for Wolf's stomach, interior

SCENE 7

On stage: Cottage set (as Scene 5)
            Various items to go into Wolf's stomach, including garden gnome
            Funnel, sparkler

Personal: **Old Lemuel:** horn
            George: large pair of scissors
            Harold: needle and thread
            Red Ridinghood: matches

LIGHTING PLOT

PROLOGUE
To open: House lights on, general stage lighting in front of gauze

Cue 1	As George and Harold arrive on stage *Fade house lights*	(Page 1)
Cue 2	**George:** "Who has asked us to meet him here." *Cut lights, lightning flashes. After a moment, bring up lights on Wolf*	(Page 1)
Cue 3	As the Wolf fades away *Bring up lights in front of gauze, fade lights behind*	(Page 2)

ACT I, SCENE 1

To open: Bright exterior lighting

Cue 4	At end of Song 2 *Dim lights slightly, occasional lightning*	(Page 8)
Cue 5	**Harold** points to darkening sky *Lightning*	(Page 8)
Cue 6	**Mr Orme:** "It's property of the bank." *Lightning*	(Page 9)
Cue 7	**Winifred:** "Oh, that's lovely." *Bring up lights*	(Page 9)
Cue 8	Jenifer, Old Lemuel and Gregory exit *Fade to Blackout*	(Page 11)

ACT I, SCENE 2

To open: The stage is dark, after a moment bring up moonlight

No cues

ACT I, SCENE 3

To open: General lighting (exterior or interior, depending on setting)

No cues

ACT I, SCENE 4

To open: Frontcloth lit

No cues

ACT I, Scene 5

To open: Bright exterior lighting

| Cue 9 | As stage empties | (Page 25) |
| | *Fade to Black-out* | |

ACT I, Scene 6

To open: Low exterior lighting

| Cue 10 | **Harold:** "Exactly, Mr Charles." | (Page 25) |
| | *Lightning* | |

| Cue 11 | **Wolf:** "... strong like an oak tree." | (Page 26) |
| | *Lightning* | |

ACT I, Scene 7

To open: Frontcloth lit

No cues

ACT I, Scene 8

To open: Exterior lighting, evening

| Cue 12 | **Red Ridinghood:** "... How do you do?" | (Page 30) |
| | *Cloud effect, lightning* | |

| Cue 13 | **Red Ridinghood:** "... How do you—" (She turns suspiciously) | (Page 30) |
| | *Lightning* | |

| Cue 14 | **Hilda:** "Stand clear while I shoot." | (Page 32) |
| | *Lightning* | |

ENTR'ACTE

To open: Gauze lit, house lights on

| Cue 15 | As George and Harold arrive on stage | (Page 33) |
| | *Fade house lights* | |

| Cue 16 | **Harold:** "... you don't know where you stand." | (Page 33) |
| | *Cut lights, lightning flashes. After a moment bring up lights on Wolf* | |

| Cue 17 | At end of Wolf Rap | (Page 34) |
| | *Fade light behind gauze, bring up lights in front* | |

ACT II, Scene 1

To open: Exterior lighting, evening

No cues

ACT II, Scene 2

To open: Frontcloth lit, evening

No cues

ACT II, Scene 3

To open: Moonlight, exterior, lantern lit as required

Cue 18   **Winifred:** "Where've they gone?"   (Page 47)
      Lightning

Cue 19   The Wolf dashes off   (Page 49)
      The light flickers

ACT II, Scene 4

To open: Frontcloth lit

No cues

ACT II, Scene 5

To open: General interior lighting

Cue 20   **Wolf:** "All the better to EAT YOU WITH!"   (Page 52)
      Lightning, then as squelching is heard, Black-out

ACT II, Scene 6

To open: Very low lighting, inside Wolf's stomach

No cues

ACT II, Scene 7

To open: Interior lighting

No cues

EFFECTS PLOT

PROLOGUE

Cue 1	**George:** "Who has asked us to meet him here."	(Page 1)
	Crash of thunder	
Cue 2	**Wolf:** "... clapped out rabbits!"	(Page 1)
	Thunder	
Cue 3	**Wolf:** "... I am still strong and sleek!"	(Page 1)
	Thunder	
Cue 4	**Wolf:** "... and get on with it!"	(Page 1)
	Thunder	
Cue 5	**Wolf:** "... to wait for youuuuuuuu!"	(Page 2)
	Thunder, fading away	

ACT I

Cue 6	**George:** "... girls especially."	(Page 4)
	Noise of argument	
Cue 7	**Jenifer:** "Oh great!"	(Page 6)
	Atmospheric music	
Cue 8	**Old Lemuel:** "There. That's it."	(Page 6)
	Cut music	
Cue 9	**Old Lemuel:** "Oh! That's not it."	(Page 6)
	Music	
Cue 10	**Old Lemuel:** "There, that's it."	(Page 7)
	Cut music	
Cue 11	At end of song 2	(Page 8)
	Thunder, a growl	
Cue 12	**George:** "... a couple of mouldy geese."	(Page 8)
	Low rumble of thunder	
Cue 13	**Mr Orme:** "It's property of the bank."	(Page 9)
	Roar, roll of thunder	
Cue 14	**Jenifer:** "... weapons and things!"	(Page 9)
	Roar	
Cue 15	At climax of booing	(Page 9)
	Roar	
Cue 16	**Winifred:** "Oh, that's lovely."	(Page 9)
	Fade roar; after a moment, bring up bird song	

ENTR'ACTE

ACT II

MADE AND PRINTED IN GREAT BRITAIN BY
LATIMER TREND & COMPANY LTD PLYMOUTH

MADE IN ENGLAND